Clothes

100 Years Ago

by Allison Lassieur

Say hello to amicus readers.

You'll find our helpful dog, Amicus, chasing a ball—to let you know the reading level of a book.

A

Learn to Read
Frequent repetition of sentence structures, high frequency words, and familiar topics provide ample support for brand new readers. Approximately 100 words.

Read Independently
Repetition is mixed with varied sentence structures and 6 to 8 content words per book are introduced with photo label and picture glossary supports. Approximately 150 words.

Read to Know More
These books feature a higher text load with additional nonfiction features such as more photos, time lines, and text divided into sections. Approximately 250 words.

Amicus Readers are published by Amicus
P.O. Box 1329, Mankato, Minnesota 56002
www.amicuspublishing.us

Printed in the United States of America at Corporate Graphics, in North Mankato, Minnesota.

Series Editor Rebecca Glaser
Series Designer Heather Dreisbach
Photo Researcher Heather Dreisbach

Photo Credits
Mary Evans Picture Library/Alamy, cover, 9, 20m; Images.com/Alamy, 1, 12; Vintage Images/Alamy, 5; FREDERICK C. HOWE/National Geographic Stock, 6; Wisconsin Historical Society, 7, 15; Vintage*Kids/Alamy, 10; McCord Museum, 11; Desiree Mueller/Photolibrary, 13; Sean Sexton/Getty Images, 14; INTERFOTO/Alamy, 17; Rue des Archives/The Granger Collection, NYC, 18; Zirconicusso/Dreamstime.com, 20t; Bill Noll/iStockphoto, 20b; Nataliia Tsukanova/Dreamstime.com, 21t; David Leindecker/iStockphoto, 21b; The Granger Collection, 21m, 22t; Goldenkb/Dreamstime.com, 22b

Library of Congress Cataloging-in-Publication Data
Lassieur, Allison.
Clothes: 100 years ago / by Allison Lassieur.
p. cm. – (Amicus Readers. 100 years ago)
Includes index.
Summary: "Discusses turn-of-the-century children's clothing and how what they wore in the early 1900s is different from what children wear today. Includes "What's Different?" photo quiz"–Provided by publisher.
ISBN 978-1-60753-163-0 (library binding)
1. Clothing and dress–History–Juvenile literature. I. Title.
GT518.L37 2012
391–dc22

2010049881

1024 3-2011
10 9 8 7 6 5 4 3 2 1

Table of Contents

100 Years Ago

Clothes one hundred years ago weren't like clothes today. Kids only had a few outfits. School clothes were made of ordinary fabrics like wool or cotton. Dressy clothes were made out of silk and linen.

Clothes for Young Kids

Little girls and boys wore dresses all the time. Boys wore dresses until they were five or six years old. Then they wore short pants. Winter dresses were made of wool. Summer dresses were made of cotton or linen.

Cotton Dress

Boys and girls wore drawers under their clothes. Drawers covered the legs down to the knees. In wintertime, everyone wore heavy wool drawers and underclothes to keep warm.

A.1463-5

Sailor suits were very popular for boys and girls. The fashion started when Queen Victoria of England dressed her boys in sailor suits. Americans copied the fashion.

Boys' swimsuits looked like pants and T-shirts. Suits for girls looked like dresses. Swimsuits were made of wool. The suits got heavy when they were wet.

Footwear was different, too. There were no sandals or sneakers. Kids wore leather shoes or boots. They also wore long stockings that went above the knee.

Leather Shoes

Clothes for Older Kids

Boys weren't allowed to wear long pants until they were teenagers. It was a big deal when a boy was old enough to wear long pants for the first time. It was a sign that he was becoming a man.

Girls' dresses reached to below their knees. When girls got older, they were allowed to wear long dresses that went to the floor. It was proof that a girl was growing up.

Photo Glossary

cotton—lightweight cloth made from the cotton plant, often used for summer clothes

drawers—long underpants worn by boys and girls one hundred years ago

linen—a cool, light fabric used for warm-weather clothes

silk—a soft, shiny cloth made from the fibers a silkworm makes

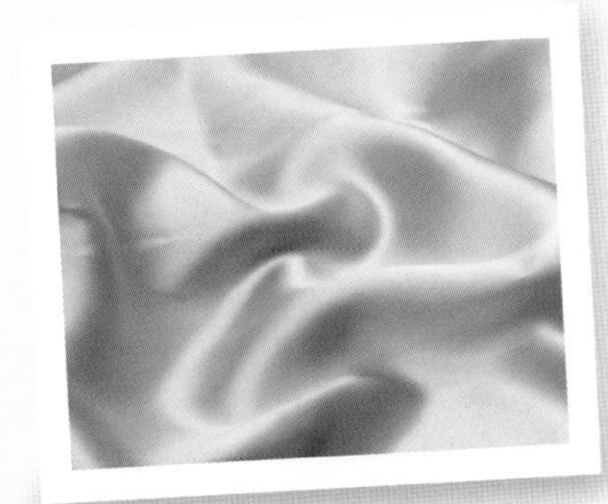

stocking—a long, thick sock

wool—heavy cloth made from the soft, thick, curly hair of sheep

What's Different?

How many differences in clothing can you find between the scene from 1910 and the scene from today?

Ideas for Parents and Teachers

100 Years Ago, an Amicus Readers Level 2 series, introduces children to everyday life around 100 years ago, in the early 1900s. Use the following strategies to help readers predict and comprehend the text.

Before Reading

- Ask the children to describe the kinds of clothes they wear every day.
- Ask about clothes that are for special occasions or certain types of weather, and how they're different from everyday clothes.

Read the Book

- Have children read the book independently.
- Encourage them to look for details in the photos.
- Remind them to look up unfamiliar words in the photo glossary.

After Reading

- Have the child explain how the clothes that children wore in the past are different than what is worn today.
- Use the What's Different? activity on page 22 to reinforce the differences.
- Encourage the child to think further by asking questions such as, "How easy would it be to play in clothes back then?" and "What clothes would you like to wear if you were a child one hundred years ago?"

Index

Children's Costume—V&A Museum of Childhood
http://www.vam.ac.uk/moc/collections/costume/index.html

Children's Costume History—Coloring Pages
http://www.fashion-era.com/Childrens_clothes/index.htm

Past Patterns: 1900-1920's Patterns
http://www.pastpatterns.com/kids.html

Wisconsin Historical Society Online Collections
http://www.wisconsinhistory.org/museum/collections/online/